BY ELIZABETH NOLL

FLYING ROBOTS

BLASTOFF!
DISCOVERY

Blastoff! Discovery launches a new mission: reading to learn. Filled with facts and features, each book offers you an exciting new world to explore!

This edition first published in 2018 by Bellwether Media, Inc.

No part of this publication may be reproduced in whole or in part without written permission of the publisher.
For information regarding permission, write to Bellwether Media, Inc., Attention: Permissions Department, 5357 Penn Avenue South, Minneapolis, MN 55419.

Library of Congress Cataloging-in-Publication Data

Names: Noll, Elizabeth, author.
Title: Flying Robots / by Elizabeth Noll.
Description: Minneapolis, MN : Bellwether Media, Inc., [2018]
   | Series: Blastoff! Discovery. World of Robots | Audience:
   Ages 7-13. | Includes bibliographical references and index.
Identifiers: LCCN 2016053594 (print) | LCCN 2016055686
   (ebook) | ISBN 9781626176881 (hardcover : alk. paper)
   | ISBN 9781681034188 (ebook) | ISBN 9781618912916
   (paperback : alk. paper)
Subjects: LCSH: Drone aircraft–Juvenile literature. | Robotics–
   Juvenile literature.
Classification: LCC UG1242.D7 N65 2018 (print) | LCC
   UG1242.D7 (ebook) | DDC 629.133/39-dc23
LC record available at https://lccn.loc.gov/2016053594

Editor: Christina Leaf   Designer: Jon Eppard

Printed in the United States of America, North Mankato, MN.

TABLE OF CONTENTS

FLYING ROBOT AT WORK!

Ramón could not move. The earthquake had knocked down his house, and he was pinned under heavy boards. He could see a tiny patch of blue sky and lots of **rubble**. There were voices in the street. Ramón tried to yell. But dust coated his throat and made it hard to speak. The voices moved away.

Much later, Ramón heard a faint sound. A small white machine flew overhead. It looked too small to hold a person but too big to be a toy.

RESCUE BOTS

After Hurricane Katrina in 2005, rescue workers in Mississippi used drones to help find survivors.

After a long time, it got dark. Ramón wondered if anyone would find him. He knew his mom would be worried. Then he heard voices again. Someone was pulling him free.

As the firefighter put Ramón in the ambulance, he told the driver that a drone had saved Ramón. It had used an **infrared camera** to take photos as it flew over the destroyed town. Ramón and three other children showed up in the photos because of their body heat. They all survived!

WHAT ARE FLYING ROBOTS?

Not all robots are stuck on the ground. Unmanned aerial vehicles, or UAVs, are robots that can fly. Many people call these robots drones.

These aircraft do not carry passengers or pilots. Most UAVs are guided by **remote** control. Others are **autonomous**. That means a computer program tells them what to do. These take off, fly a route, perform tasks, and land on their own.

Flying robots have many uses. Some search for survivors after natural disasters like earthquakes and floods. Others map oil spills and other forms of **pollution**.

Some flying robots do things in place of police or soldiers. They enter dangerous situations like angry crowds so police do not have to. UAVs also save military lives by locating **land mines**.

Many military drones shoot **missiles** and bullets. They target dangerous enemy leaders without risking soldiers' lives.

MQ-9 Reaper firing missiles

ARMED AND DANGEROUS?

Some people are against using armed UAVs in the military. They argue that these drones often harm innocent people.

Consumer drones are fairly small and affordable. Many people fly them just for fun. Others use them to take aerial photos or help with projects. Some channels show drone races on TV. Many drones in these races are called **quadcopters**.

drone race

Companies use drones, too. Moviemakers in production companies use them to get aerial shots. Stores and online companies want to use UAVs to deliver packages. In the future, drones may deliver things that people order on the Internet.

WHAT A DEAL!

A helicopter shoot for a film can cost $25,000 a day. A filmmaker can rent a drone, with ground crew, for $5,000 a day.

THE DEVELOPMENT OF
FLYING ROBOTS

An early version of remote aerial warfare appeared during World War I. In 1918, Charles Kettering built the Kettering Bug. This small, single-use plane was designed to carry a bomb but no pilot.

Charles Kettering

The first returnable UAV was the Queen Bee in World War II. Britain used these radio-controlled **biplanes** for target practice. The United States and Germany also began to use unmanned bombers in the last two years of the war.

DRONE BEGINNINGS

The name "drone" was likely inspired by the Queen Bee. Drones are male bees that follow the queen bee in a hive.

Kettering Bug

Queen Bee

MQ-1 Predator drone

UAVs became more advanced in the decades after WWII. In the 1960s, the U.S. Army and Navy used the QH-50 DASH (Drone Anti-Submarine Helicopter). In the 1970s and 1980s, the Israeli military used the Tadiran Mastiff and IAI Scout for **surveillance**.

In 1995, the U.S. launched the MQ-1 Predator drone. The U.S. has used this battle drone in combat in many countries, mainly in the **Middle East**. Today, about one out of every three U.S. military aircraft are UAVs.

QH-50 DASH

Tadiran Mastiff

RQ-4 Global Hawk

Today, UAVs are also used for much more than just the military. People use drones for important tasks in business. Scientists use them for research. Quadcopters like the DJI Phantom are popular with people just wanting to have fun. In early 2016, there were about 2.5 million consumer drones in the U.S.!

DJI Phantom

The technology for UAVs continues to get better as computers get more advanced. This has led to UAVs of all shapes and sizes. Some UAVs have wingspans smaller than 2 inches (5 centimeters). Others are huge. The U.S. military's Global Hawk has a wingspan of 130.9 feet (39.9 meters)!

SKEYE Nano 2 FPV

FLYING ROBOT PROFILE: CAMCOPTER S-100

The Camcopter S-100 is an autonomous drone. It can take off, fly its mission, return, and land without being guided by remote control. A computer program tells it where to go and what to do. A human on the ground can take control if need be.

Schiebel, a company in Austria, created the S-100 around 2005. Many countries have purchased the robots for their militaries, including the U.S., Germany, India, and China. But the S-100 has non-military uses, too, including mapping and farming.

Name:	Camcopter S-100
Developer:	Schiebel Corporation
Release Date:	2006
Functions:	search and rescue, surveillance, photography, mapping, border patrol
Size:	10.2 feet (3.1 meters) long; 4 feet (1.2 meters) wide; and 3.7 feet (1.1 meters) high
Speed:	138 miles (222 kilometers) per hour
Range:	124 miles (200 kilometers)

A COSTLY COPTER

The Camcopter S-100 costs about $400,000.

FLYING ROBOT PROFILE: PARROT MAMBO

The Parrot Mambo is a user-friendly **minidrone**. Like other quadcopters, it has four rotors that lift the drone and move it. The rotors make the Parrot Mambo a skilled flier. It can do loops, flips, and sharp turns. It will also start its engine automatically when thrown into the air!

The Parrot Mambo can do more than just fly. It comes with two accessories. One is a cannon that shoots tiny plastic balls. The other is a grabber arm. The grabber arm can pick up light things, like a dollar bill or a paperclip.

grabber arm

Name:	Parrot Mambo
Developer:	Parrot
Release Date:	2016
Functions:	fly and play
Size:	7.1 inches (18 centimeters) by 7.1 inches (18 centimeters) with bumpers
Speed:	18 miles (29 kilometers) per hour
Range:	up to 65 feet (19.8 meters) with app, 196 feet (60 meters) with the Parrot Flypad (remote control)

cannon

FLYING ROBOT PROFILE:
MQ-1 PREDATOR

The Predator is one of the most well-known military drones. It was first used for surveillance and **reconnaissance**. It had cameras and **sensors** that sent images back to the operator. Then in 2001, it was armed with Hellfire missiles. After that, the Predator flew many attack missions over Afghanistan and nearby countries. In 2011, new MQ-9 Reapers began to replace the Predator.

The Predator's crew was usually in the U.S., thousands of miles away. One person remotely controlled the craft's movement. Another person controlled the sensors and missiles.

Name:	MQ-1 Predator
Developer:	General Atomics Aeronautical Systems
Release Date:	1995
Functions:	reconnaissance, surveillance, precision strike
Size:	27 feet (8.2 meters) long; 7 feet (2.1 meters) high; wingspan of 49 feet (15 meters)
Speed:	135 miles (217 kilometers) per hour
Range:	770 miles (1,239 kilometers); can stay up for 24 hours

Hellfire missiles

FIREFIGHTING DRONES

In 2013, a Predator helped fight a huge California wildfire. The drone flew over the area to get video images of the fire. These helped ground crews stop the fire's spread and get out safely.

FLYING ROBOT PROFILE: MATTERNET M2

Delivery drones are not yet reality in the U.S. Laws state that people who fly **commercial** drones have to be able to see their drones at all times. But a company called Matternet has tested their M2 delivery drone in Haiti, Switzerland, and other countries. This quadcopter carries small packages, including medical supplies, to areas that are hard to reach.

Recently, M2s became part of a drone delivery system with Mercedes-Benz vans. The drones fly to and from the van's roof.

Name:	Matternet M2
Nickname:	M2
Developer:	Matternet
Release Date:	September 7, 2016
Function:	delivery
Size:	31.4 inches (80 centimeters) long; 31.4 inches (80 centimeters) wide; 10.2 inches (26 centimeters) tall
Speed:	about 26.8 miles (43.1 kilometers) per hour
Range:	12 miles (19 kilometers)

MONTHLY RENT

Even if the laws change, buying an M2 to go get the groceries will probably not be practical. The cost could be $1,000 per month to rent!

THE FUTURE OF FLYING ROBOTS

More people buy flying robots each year. The Federal Aviation Administration (FAA) predicts that by 2020, about 7 million drones will be flying U.S. skies. Roughly one out of every three will be used by companies. Drone racers and other hobbyists will probably own more than 4 million drones.

Many people have concerns about the increasing number of flying robots. They worry drones could invade privacy or add more noise to the world. However, the soaring popularity of flying robots suggests they are here to stay.

LICENSE TO FLY

In 2015, the FAA began requiring owners to register drones between 0.55 and 55 pounds (0.25 and 25 kilograms). But it is believed that less than half of all drones are registered.

GLOSSARY

autonomous—able to act without help

biplanes—airplanes with two wings on each side, usually placed above one another

commercial—designed to make money

consumer—related to people who buy and use goods

infrared camera—a camera that forms an image based on the infrared radiation, usually heat, that objects give off

land mines—bombs hidden in the ground that are set off by footsteps or other weight

Middle East—a region of southwestern Asia and northern Africa; this region includes Egypt, Iran, Iraq, Israel, and other nearby countries.

minidrone—a drone that is very small and light

missiles—objects used as weapons that are launched to hit something far away

pollution—substances that make an area dirty and not safe for use

quadcopters—helicopter-style drones that are propelled by four rotors

reconnaissance—the action of exploring an area to get information

remote—far removed in place or time

rubble—broken pieces of brick, stone, or other materials from a fallen building

sensors—devices that respond to light, pressure, sound, or other physical changes

surveillance—the action of keeping a close watch on someone or something

TO LEARN MORE

AT THE LIBRARY

Dougherty, Martin J. *Drones: An Illustrated Guide to the Unmanned Aircraft That Are Filling Our Skies.* New York, N.Y.: Metro Books, 2015.

Marsico, Katie. *Drones.* New York, N.Y.: Children's Press, 2016.

Ventura, Marne. *The 12 Biggest Breakthroughs in Robot Technology.* North Mankato, Minn.: 12-Story Library, 2015.

ON THE WEB

Learning more about flying robots is as easy as 1, 2, 3.

1. Go to www.factsurfer.com.

2. Enter "flying robots" into the search box.

3. Click the "Surf" button and you will see a list of related web sites.

With factsurfer.com, finding more information is just a click away.

INDEX